W. H. AUDEN

Poems
(1930)

———

ff

faber and faber

First published in the UK in 1930
by Faber and Faber Ltd
Bloomsbury House
74–77 Great Russell Street
London WC1B 3DA

Second edition (revised) 1933
This paperback edition first published in 2013

Typeset by CB editions, London
Printed in England by T. J. International Ltd, Padstow, Cornwall

A CIP record for this book
is available from the British Library

ISBN 978-0-571-28351-4

821 AUD

2 4 6 8 10 9 7 5 3 1

Contents

Paid on Both Sides: A CHARADE 1

PAID ON BOTH SIDES
A CHARADE

TO
Cecil Day-Lewis

Characters

Lintzgarth
JOHN NOWER
DICK
GEORGE****
WALTER
KURT
CULLEY
STEPHEN**
ZEPPEL – John Nower's servant
NO. 6
JOAN – mother of John Nower
TRUDY***

Nattrass
AARON SHAW*****
SETH SHAW
THE SPY – Seth's brother
BERNARD
SETH'S MOTHER
ANNE SHAW

FATHER XMAS*
THE DOCTOR
BO****
PO*****
THE MAN-WOMAN
THE DOCTOR'S BOY**
THE ANNOUNCER*
THE CHIEF GUEST*
THE BUTLER*

THE CHORUS

The asterisked parts should be doubled

[*No scenery is required. The stage should have a curtained-off recess. The distinction between the two hostile parties should be marked by different coloured arm-bands. The chorus, which should not consist of more than three persons, wear similar and distinctive clothing.*]

[*Enter Trudy and Walter.*]

T. You've only just heard?

W. Yes. A breakdown at the Mill needed attention, kept me all morning. I guessed no harm. But lately, riding at leisure, Dick met me, panted disaster. I came here at once. How did they get him?

T. In Kettledale above Colefangs road passes where high banks overhang dangerous from ambush. To Colefangs had to go, would speak with Layard, Jerry and Hunter with him only. They must have stolen news, for Red Shaw waited with ten, so Jerry said, till for last time unconscious. Hunter was killed at first shot. They fought, exhausted ammunition, a brave defence but fight no more.

W. Has Joan been told yet?

T. Yes. It couldn't be helped. Shock, starting birth pangs, caused a premature delivery.

W. How is she?

T. Bad, I believe. But here's the doctor.

[*Enter Doctor.*]

Well, Doctor, how are things going?

D. Better, thanks. We've had a hard fight, but it's going to be all right. She'll pull through and have a fine infant as well. My God, I'm thirsty after all that. Where can I get a drink?

[5]

W.   Here in the next room, Doctor.
[*Exeunt. Back curtains draw. Joan with child and corpse.*]
J.   Not from this life, not from this life is any
           To keep; sleep, day and play would not help there
           Dangerous to new ghost; new ghost learns from
                     many
           Learns from old termers what death is, where.

           Who's jealous of his latest company
           From one day to the next final to us,
           A changed one; would use sorrow to deny
           Sorrow, to replace death; sorrow is sleeping thus.

           Unforgetting is not to-day's forgetting
           For yesterday, not bedrid scorning,
           But a new begetting
           An unforgiving morning.
[*Baby squeals.*]
           O see, he is impatient
           To pass beyond this pretty lisping time:
           There'll be some crying out when he's come there.
[*Back curtains close.*]
Chorus. Can speak of trouble, pressure on men
           Born all the time, brought forward into light
           For warm dark moan.
           Though heart fears all heart cries for, rebuffs with
                     mortal beat
           Skyfall, the legs sucked under, adder's bite.
           That prize held out of reach
           Guides the unwilling tread,
           The asking breath,
           Till on attended bed
           Or in untracked dishonour comes to each
           His natural death.

[6]

We pass our days
Speak, man to men, easy, learning to point
To jump before ladies, to show our scars:
But no
We were mistaken, these faces are not ours.
They smile no more when we smile back:
Eyes, ears, tongue, nostrils bring
News of revolt, inadequate counsel to
An infirm king.

O watcher in the dark, you wake
Our dream of waking, we feel
Your finger on the flesh that has been skinned,
By your bright day
See clear what we were doing, that we were vile.
Your sudden hand
Shall humble great
Pride, break it, wear down to stumps old systems
           which await
The last transgression of the sea.

[*Enter John Nower and Dick.*]

J.   If you have really made up your mind, Dick, I won't try and persuade you to stop. But I shall be sorry to lose you.

D.   I have thought it all over and I think it is the best thing to do. My cousin writes that the ranch is a thoroughly good proposition. I don't know how I shall like the Colonies but I feel I must get away from here. There is not room enough . . . but the actual moving is unpleasant.

J.   I understand. When are you thinking of sailing?

D.   My cousin is sailing to-morrow. If I am going I am to join him at the Docks.

J.   Right. Tell one of the men to go down to the post-

office and send a wire for you. If you want anything
else, let me know.

D.   Thank you.

[*Exit Dick. Enter Zeppel.*]

Z.   Number Six wishes to see you, sir.

J.   All right, show him in.

[*Enter Number Six.*]

         Well, what is it?

6.   My area is Rookhope. Last night at Horse and Far
rier, drank alone, one of Shaw's men. I sat down
friendly next, till muzzed with drink and lateness he
was blabbing. Red Shaw goes to Brandon Walls to-
day, visits a woman.

J.   Alone?

6.   No, Sir. He takes a few. I got no numbers.

J.   This is good news. Here is a pound for you.

6.   Thank you very much, sir.

[*Exit Number Six.*]

J.   Zeppel.

Z.   Sir.

J.   Ask George to come here at once.

Z.   Very good, sir.

[*John gets a map out. Enter George.*]

J.   Red Shaw is spending the day at Brandon Walls.
We must get him. You know the ground well, don't
you, George?

G.   Pretty well. Let me see the map. There's a barn about
a hundred yards from the house. Yes, here it is. If we
can occupy that without attracting attention it will
form a good base for operations, commands both
house and road. If I remember rightly, on the other
side of the stream is a steep bank. Yes, you can see
from the contours. They couldn't get out that way,

but lower down is marshy ground and possible. You want to post some men there to catch those who try.

J.   Good. Who do you suggest to lead that party?

G.   Send Sturton. He knows the whole district blindfold. He and I as boys fished all those streams together.

J.   I shall come with you. Let's see: it's dark now about five. Fortunately there's no moon and it's cloudy. We'll start then about half-past. Pick your men and get some sandwiches made up in the kitchen. I'll see about the ammunition if you will remember to bring a compass. We meet outside at a quarter past.

[*Exeunt. Enter Kurt and Culley.*]

K.   There's time for a quick one before changing. What's yours?

C.   I'll have a sidecar, thanks.

K.   Zeppel, one sidecar and one C.P.S. I hear Chapman did the lake in eight.

C.   Yes, he is developing a very pretty style. I am not sure though that Pepys won't beat him next year if he can get out of that double kick. Thanks. Prosit.

K.   Cheerio.

[*Enter Walter and Trudy.*]

W.   Two half pints, Zeppel, please. [*To Kurt.*] Can you let me have a match? How is the Rugger going?

K.   All right, thank you. We have not got a bad team this season.

W.   Where do you play yourself?

K.   Wing 3Q.

W.   Did you ever see Warner? No, he'd be before your time. You remember him don't you, Trudy?

T.   He was killed in the fight at Colefangs, wasn't he?

W.   You are muddling him up with Hunter. He was the best three-quarter I have ever seen. His sprinting was marvellous to watch.

Z. [*producing Christmas turkey*] Not bad eh?

T. [*feeling it*] Oh a fine one. For to-morrow's dinner?

Z.   Yes. Here, puss . . . gobble, gobble . . .

T. [*to W.*] What have you got Ingo for Christmas?

W.   A model crane. Do you think he will like it?

T.   He loves anything mechanical. He's so excited he can't sleep.

K.   Come on, Culley, finish your drink. We must be getting along. [*To W.*] You must come down to the field on Monday and see us.

W.   I will if I can.

[*Exit Kurt and Culley.*]

T.   Is there any news yet?

W.   Nothing has come through. If things are going right they may be back any time now.

T.   I suppose they will get him?

W.   It's almost certain. Nower has waited long enough.

T.   I am sick of this feud. What do we want to go on killing each other for? We are all the same. He's trash, yet if I cut my finger it bleeds like his. But he's swell, keeps double shifts working all night by flares. His mother squealed like a pig when he came crouching out.

Sometimes we read a sign, cloud in the sky,
The wet tracks of a hare, quicken the step
Promise the best day. But here no remedy
Is to be thought of, no news but the new death;
A Nower dragged out in the night, a Shaw
Ambushed behind the wall. Blood on the ground
Would welcome fighters. Last night at Hammergill
A boy was born fanged like a weasel. I am old,
Shall die before next winter, but more than once
          shall hear

The cry for help, the shooting round the house.

W.   The best are gone.
Often the man, alone shut, shall consider
The killings in old winters, death of friends.
Sitting with stranger shall expect no good.

Spring came, urging to ships, a casting off,
But one would stay, vengeance not done; it seemed
Doubtful to them that they would meet again.

Fording in the cool of the day they rode
To meet at crossroads when the year was over:
Dead is Brody, such a man was Maul.

I will say this not falsely; I have seen
The just and the unjust die in the day,
All, willing or not, and some were willing.

Here they are.
[*Enter Nower, George, Sturton and others. The three speak
alternately.*]

Day was gone Night covered sky
Black over earth When we came there
To Brandon Walls Where Red Shaw lay
Hateful and sleeping Unfriendly Visit.
I wished to revenge Quit fully
Who my father at Colefangs valley
Lying in ambush Cruelly shot
With life for life.

Then watchers saw they were attacked
Shouted in fear A night alarm
To men asleep Doomed men awoke
Felt for their guns Ran to the doors
Would wake their master Who lay with woman

Upstairs together Tired after love.
He saw then There would be shooting
Hard fight.

Shot answered shot Bullets screamed
Guns shook Hot in the hand
Fighters lay Groaning on ground
Gave up life Edward fell
Shot through the chest First of our lot
By no means refused fight Stephen was good
His first encounter Showed no fear
Wounded many.

Then Shaw knew We were too strong
Would get away Over the moor
Return alive But found at the ford
Sturton waiting Greatest gun anger
There he died Nor any came
Fighters home Nor wives shall go
Smiling to bed They boast no more.

[*Stephen suddenly gets up.*]

S.   A forward forward can never be a backward backward.

G.   Help me put Stephen to bed, somebody. He got tight on the way back. Hullo, they've caught a spy.

Voices outside: Look out. There he is. Catch him. Got you.

[*Enter Kurt and others with prisoner.*]

K.   We found this chap hiding in an outhouse.

J.   Bring him here. Who are you?

S.   I know him. I saw him once at Eickhamp. He's Seth Shaw's brother.

J.   He is, is he. What do you come here for? You know what we do to spies. I'll destroy the whole lot of you.

Take him out.

Spy. You may look big, but we'll get you one day, Nower.
[*Exeunt all but John, Stephen following.*]

S. Don't go, darling.
[*John sits. A shot outside followed by cheers.*]
[*Enter Zeppel.*]

Z. Will you be wanting anything more to-night, Sir?

J. No, that will be all thank you.

Z. Good night, sir.

John. Always the following wind of history
Of others' wisdom makes a buoyant air
Till we come suddenly on pockets where
Is nothing loud but us; where voices seem
Abrupt, untrained, competing with no lie
Our fathers shouted once. They taught us war,
To scamper after darlings, to climb hills,
To emigrate from weakness, find ourselves
The easy conquerors of empty bays:
But never told us this, left each to learn,
Hear something of that soon-arriving day
When to gaze longer and delighted on
A face or idea be impossible.
Could I have been some simpleton that lived
Before disaster sent his runners here;
Younger than worms, worms have too much to bear.
Yes, mineral were best: could I but see
These woods, these fields of green, this lively world
Sterile as moon.

Chorus. The Spring unsettles sleeping partnerships,
Foundries improve their casting process, shops
Open a further wing on credit till
The winter. In summer boys grow tall
With running races on the froth-wet sand,

War is declared there, here a treaty signed;
Here a scrum breaks up like a bomb, there troops '
Deploy like birds. But proudest into traps
Have fallen. These gears which ran in oil for week
By week, needing no look, now will not work;
Those manors mortgaged twice to pay for love
Go to another.

        O how shall man live
Whose thought is born, child of one farcical night,
To find him old? The body warm but not
By choice, he dreams of folk in dancing bunches,
Of tart wine spilt on home-made benches,
Where learns, one drawn apart, a secret will
Restore the dead; but comes thence to a wall.
Outside on frozen soil lie armies killed
Who seem familiar but they are cold.
Now the most solid wish he tries to keep
His hands show through; he never will look up,
Say 'I am good'. On him misfortune falls
More than enough. Better where no one feels,
The out-of-sight, buried too deep for shafts.

[*Enter Father Christmas. He speaks to the audience.*]

X.   Ladies and Gentlemen: I should like to thank you all
very much for coming here to-night. Now we have a
little surprise for you. When you go home, I hope you
will tell your friends to come and bring the kiddies,
but you will remember to keep this a secret, won't
you? Thank you. Now I will not keep you waiting
any longer.

[*Lights. A trial. John as the accuser. The Spy as accused. Joan
as his warder with a gigantic feeding bottle. Xmas as presi-
dent, the rest as jury, wearing school caps.*]

X.   Is there any more evidence?

J.   Yes. I know we have and are making terrific sacri-
fices, but we cannot give in. We cannot betray the
dead. As we pass their graves can we be deaf to the
simple eloquence of their inscriptions, those who in
the glory of their early manhood gave up their lives
for us? No, we must fight to the finish.

X.   Very well. Call the witness.

[*Enter Bo.*]

B.   In these days during the migrations, days
Freshening with rain reported from the mountains,
By loss of memory we are reborn,
For memory is death; by taking leave,
Parting in anger and glad to go
Where we are still unwelcome, and if we count
What dead the tides wash in, only to make
Notches for enemies. On northern ridges
Where flags fly, seen and lost, denying rumour
We baffle proof, speakers of a strange tongue.

[*The Spy groans. His cries are produced by jazz instruments
at the back of the stage. Joan brandishes her bottle.*]

Joan.   Be quiet, or I'll give you a taste of this.

X.   Next, please.

[*Enter Po.*]

P.   Past victory is honour, to accept
An island governorship, back to estates
Explored as child; coming at last to love
Lost publicly, found secretly again
In private flats, admitted to a sign.
An understanding sorrow knows no more,
Sits waiting for the lamp, far from those hills
Where rifts open unfenced, mark of a fall,
And flakes fall softly softly burying

Deeper and deeper down her loving son.

[*The Spy groans. John produces a revolver.*]

J.   Better to get it over.

Joan. This way for the Angel of Peace.

X.   Leave him alone. This fellow is very very ill.
        But he will get well.

[*The Man-Woman appears as a prisoner of war behind barbed wire, in the snow.*]

M-W. Because I'm come it does not mean to hold
        An anniversary, think illness healed,
        As to renew the lease, consider costs
        Of derelict ironworks on deserted coasts.
        Love was not love for you but episodes,
        Traffic in memoirs, views from different sides;
        You thought oaths of comparison a bond,
        And though you had your orders to disband,
        Refused to listen, but remained in woods
        Poorly concealed your profits under wads.
        Nothing was any use; therefore I went
        Hearing you call for what you did not want.
        I lay with you; you made that an excuse
        For playing with yourself, but homesick because
        Your mother told you that's what flowers did,
        And thought you lived since you were bored, not
                dead,
        And could not stop. So I was cold to make
        No difference, but you were quickly meek
        Altered for safety. I tried then to demand
        Proud habits, protestations called your mind
        To show you it was extra, but instead
        You overworked yourself, misunderstood,
        Adored me for the chance. Lastly I tried
        To teach you acting, but always you had nerves

To fear performances as some fear knives.
Now I shall go. No, you, if you come,
Will not enjoy yourself, for where I am
All talking is forbidden. . . .

[*The Spy groans.*]

J.   I can't bear it.

[*Shoots him. Lights out.*]

Voices. Quick, fetch a doctor.
        Ten pounds for a doctor.
        Ten pounds to keep him away.
        Coming, coming.

[*Lights. Xmas, John and the Spy remain. The jury has gone,
but there is a Photographer.*]

X.   Stand back there. Here comes the doctor.

[*Enter Doctor and his Boy.*]

B.   Tickle your arse with a feather, sir.

D.   What's that?

B.   Particularly nasty weather, sir.

D.   Yes, it is. Tell me, is my hair tidy? One must always be
       careful with a new client.

B.   It's full of lice, sir.

D.   What's that?

B.   It's looking nice, sir.

[*For the rest of the scene the boy fools about.*]

X.   Are you the doctor?

D.   I am.

X.   What can you cure?

D.   Tennis elbow, Graves' Disease, Derbyshire neck and
       Housemaid's knees.

X.   Is that all you can cure?

D.   No, I have discovered the origin of life. Fourteen
       months I hesitated before I concluded this diagnosis.
       I received the morning star for this. My head will be

[17]

left at death for clever medical analysis. The laugh
will be gone and the microbe in command.

X.   Well, let's see what you can do.

[*Doctor takes circular saws, bicycle pumps, etc., from his
bag.*]

B.   You need a pill, sir.

D.   What's that.

B.   You'll need your skill, sir. O sir you're hurting.

[*Boy is kicked out.*]

[*John tries to get a look.*]

D.   Go away. Your presence will be necessary at Scot-
land Yard when the criminals of the war are tried, but
your evidence will not be needed. It is valueless.
Cages will be provided for some of the more interest-
ing specimens. [*Examines the body.*] Um, yes. Very
interesting. The conscious brain appears normal ex-
cept under emotion. Fancy it. The Devil couldn't do
that. This advances and retreats under control and
poisons everything round it. My diagnosis is: Ada-
mant will, cool brain and laughing spirit. Hullo,
what's this? [*Produces a large pair of pliers and ex-
tracts an enormous tooth from the body.*] Come
along, that's better. Ladies and Gentlemen, you see I
have nothing up my sleeve. This tooth was growing
ninety-nine years before his great grandmother was
born. If it hadn't been taken out to-day he would have
died yesterday. You may get up now.

[*The Spy gets up. The Photographer gets ready.*]

P.   Just one minute, please. A little brighter, a little bright-
er. No, moisten the lips and start afresh. Hold it.

[*Photographer lets off his flash. Lights out. Xmas blows a
whistle.*]

X.   All change.

[*Lights. Spy behind a gate guarded by Xmas. Enter John running.*]

J.   I'm late, I'm late. Which way is it? I must hurry.

X.   You can't come in here, without a pass.

[*John turns back his coat lapel.*]

X.   O I beg your pardon, sir. This way, sir.

[*Exit Xmas. The Accuser and Accused plant a tree.*]

John.   Sametime sharers of the same house
          We know not the builder nor the name of his son.
          Now cannot mean to them; boy's voice among
                    dishonoured portraits
          To dockside barmaid speaking
          Sorry through wires, pretended speech.

Spy.   Escaped
          Armies pursuit, rebellion and eclipse
          Together in a cart
          After all journeys
          We stay and are not known.

[*Lights out.*]

          Sharers of the same house
          Attendants on the same machine
          Rarely a word, in silence understood.

[*Lights. John alone in his chair. Enter Dick.*]

D.   Hullo. I've come to say good-bye.
          Yesterday we sat at table together
          Fought side by side at enemies face to face meeting
          To-day we take our leave, time of departure.
          I'm sorry.

J.   Here, give me your knife and take mine. By these
          We may remember each other.
          There are two chances, but more of one
          Parting for ever, not hearing the other
          Though he need help.

Have you got everything you want?

D.   Yes, thanks. Goodbye, John.

J.   Goodbye.

[*Exit Dick.*]

>There is the city,
>Lighted and clean once, pleasure for builders
>And I
>Letting to cheaper tenants, have made a slum
>Houses at which the passer shakes his fist
>Remembering evil.
>Pride and indifference have shared with me, and I
>Have kissed them in the dark, for mind has dark,
>Shaded commemorations, midnight accidents
>In streets where heirs may dine.
>
>But love, sent east for peace
>From tunnels under those
>Bursts now to pass
>On trestles over meaner quarters
>A noise and flashing glass.
>
>Feels morning streaming down
>Wind from the snows
>Nowise withdrawn by doubting flinch
>Nor joined to any by belief's firm flange
>Refreshed sees all
>The tugged-at teat
>The hopper's steady feed, the frothing leat.
>Zeppel.

[*Enter Zeppel.*]

Z.   Sir.

J.   Get my horse ready at once, please.

[*Exeunt.*]

Chorus. To throw away the key and walk away

Not abrupt exile, the neighbours asking why,
But following a line with left and right
An altered gradient at another rate
Learns more than maps upon the whitewashed wall
The hand put up to ask; and makes us well
Without confession of the ill. All pasts
Are single old past now, although some posts
Are forwarded, held looking on a new view;
The future shall fulfil a surer vow
Not smiling at queen over the glass rim
Nor making gunpowder in the top room,
Not swooping at the surface still like gulls
But with prolonged drowning shall develop gills.

But there are still to tempt; areas not seen
Because of blizzards or an erring sign
Whose guessed at wonders would be worth alleging,
And lies about the cost of a night's lodging.
Travellers may sleep at inns but not attach,
They sleep one night together, not asked to touch;
Receive no normal welcome, not the pressed lip,
Children to lift, not the assuaging lap.
Crossing the pass descend the growing stream
Too tired to hear except the pulses' strum,
Reach villages to ask for a bed in
Rock shutting out the sky, the old life done.

[*Culley enters right and squats in the centre of the stage,
looking left through field glasses. Several shots are heard off.
Enter George and Kurt.*]

G.   Are you much hurt?
K.   Nothing much, sir. Only a slight flesh wound. Did
      you get him, sir?
G.   On ledge above the gulley, aimed at, seen moving,
      fell; looked down on, sprawls in the stream.

[21]

K.   Good. He sniped poor Billy last Easter, riding to Flash.

G.   I have some lint and bandages in my haversack, and there is a spring here. I'll dress your arm.

[*Enter Seth finds Bernard, left.*]

S.   Did you find Tom's body?

B.   Yes, Sir. It's lying in the Hangs.

S.   Which way did they go?

B.   Down there, sir.

[*Culley observes them and runs right.*]

C.   There are twenty men from Nattrass, sir, over the gap, coming at once.

G.   Have they seen us?

C.   Not yet.

G.   We must get out. You go down to the copse and make for the Barbon road. We'll follow the old tramway. Keep low and run like hell.

[*Exeunt right. Seth watches through field glasses.*]

S.   Yes. No. No. Yes, I can see them. They are making for the Barbon road. Go down and cut them off. There is good cover by the bridge. We've got them now.

[*A whistle. The back curtains draw, showing John, Anne and Aaron and the Announcer grouped. Both sides enter left and right.*]

Aa.   There is a time for peace; too often we
        Have gone on cold marches, have taken life,
        Till wrongs are bred like flies; the dreamer wakes
        Who beats a smooth door, behind footsteps, on the
                left
        The pointed finger, the unendurable drum,
        To hear of horses stolen or a house burned.
        Now this shall end with marriage as it ought:

Love turns the wind, brings up the salt smell,
Shadow of gulls on the road to the sea.

Announcer. The engagement is announced of John Nower, eldest son of the late Mr. and Mrs. George Nower of Lintzgarth, Rockhope, and Anne Shaw, only daughter of the late Mr. and Mrs. Joseph Shaw of Nattrass, Garrigill.

All.   Hurrah.

[*George and Seth advance to the centre, shake hands and cross over the stage to their opposite sides. Back curtains close. Exeunt in different directions, talking as they go.*]

G.   It was a close shave that time. We had a lucky escape. How are you feeling?

K.   The arm is rather painful. I owe Bernard one for that.

B.   It's a shame. Just when we had them fixed.

S.   Don't you worry. You'll get your chance.

B.   But what about this peace?

S.   That remains to be seen. Only wait.

[*Exeunt. Back curtains draw. John and Anne alone. John blows on a grass held between the thumbs and listens.*]

J.   On Cautley where a peregrine has nested, iced heather hurt the knuckles. Fell on the ball near time, the forward stopped. Good-bye now, he said, would open the swing doors. . . . These I remember, but not love till now. We cannot tell where we shall find it, though we all look for it till we do, and what others tell us is no use to us.

Some say that handsome raider still at large,
A terror to the Marshes, is truth in love;
And we must listen for such messengers
To tell us daily 'To-day a saint came blessing
The huts.' 'Seen lately in the provinces

Reading behind a tree and people passing.'
But love returns;
At once all heads are turned this way, and love
Calls order – silenced the angry sons –
Steps forward, greets, repeats what he has heard
And seen, feature for feature, word for word.

Anne. Yes, I am glad this evening that we are together.
The silence is unused, death seems
        An axe's echo.

The summer quickens all,
Scatters its promises
To you and me no less
Though neither can compel.

J. The wish to last the year,
The longest look to live,
The urgent word survive
The movement of the air.

A. But loving now let none
Think of divided days
When we shall choose from ways,
All of them evil, one.

J. Look on with stricter brows
The sacked and burning town,
The ice-sheet moving down,
The fall of an old house.

A. John, I have a car waiting. There is time to join Dick
before the boat sails. We sleep in beds where men
have died howling.

J. You may be right, but we shall stay.

A. To-night the many come to mind
Sent forward in the thaw with anxious marrow
For such might now return with a bleak face,

An image pause half-lighted in the door,
A greater but not fortunate in all;
Come home deprived of an astonishing end . . .
Morgan's who took a clean death in the north
Shouting against the wind, or Cousin Dodd's,
Passed out in her chair, the snow falling.
The too-loved clays, born ever by diverse drifts,
Fallen upon the far side of all enjoyment,
Unable to move closer, shall not speak
Out of that grave stern on no capital fault;
Enough to have lightly touched the unworthy thing.

J. We live still.

A. But what has become of the dead? They forget.

J. These. Smilers, all who stand on promontories, slinkers, whisperers, deliberate approaches, echoes, time, promises of mercy, what dreams or goes masked, embraces that fail, insufficient evidence, touches of the old wound.

But let us not think of things which we hope will be long in coming.

Chorus. The Spring will come,
Not hesitate for one employer who
Though a fine day and every pulley running
Would quick lie down; nor save the wanted one
That, wounded in escaping; swam the lake
Safe to the reeds, collapsed in shallow water.
You have tasted good and what is it? For you,
Sick in the green plain, healed in the tundra, shall
Turn westward back from your alone success,
Under a dwindling Alp to see your friends
Cut down the wheat.

J. It's getting cold dear, let's go in.

[Exeunt. Back curtains close.]

*Chorus.*For where are Basley who won the Ten,
Dickon so tasted by the House,
Thomas who kept a sparrow-hawk?

The clock strikes, it is time to go,
The tongue ashamed, deceived by a shake of the
hand.

[*Enter Bridal Party left, guests right.*]

Guests. Ssh.

[*The Chief Guest comes forward and presents a bouquet to
the bride.*]

C.G. With gift in hand we come
From every neighbour farm
To celebrate in wine
The certain union of
A woman and a man;
And may their double love
Be shown to the stranger's eye
In a son's symmetry.
Now hate is swallowed down,
All anger put away;
The spirit comes to its own,
The beast to its play.

[*All clap. The Chief Guest addresses the Audience.*]

C.G. Will any lady be so kind as to oblige us with a dance?
. . . Thank you very much . . . This way miss . . . What
tune would you like?

[*Gramophone. A dance. As the dance ends, the back curtains
draw and the Butler enters centre.*]

Butler. Dinner is served.

[*Aaron goes to the Dancer.*]

Aa. You'll dine with us, of course?

[*Exeunt all except Seth and his Mother.*]

[*Guests, as they go out.*] It will be a good year for them, I
    think.
    You don't mean that he . . . well, you know what.
    Rather off his form lately.
    The vein is showing good in the Quarry Hazel.
    One of Edward's friends.
    You must come and have a look at the Kennels some
    day.
    Well it does seem to show.
            [*Etc., etc.*]
[*Back curtains close.*]
Mother. Seth.
S.   Yes, Mother.
M.   John Nower is here.
S.   I know that. What do you want me to do?
M.   Kill him.
S.   I can't do that. There is peace now; besides he is a
        guest in our house.
M.   Have you forgotten your brother's death . . . taken
        out and shot like a dog? It is a nice thing for me to
        hear people saying that I have a coward for a son. I
        am thankful your father is not here to see it.
S.   I'm not afraid of anything or anybody, but I don't
        want to.
M.   I shall have to take steps.
S.   It shall be as you like. Though I think that much will
        come of this, chiefly harm.
M.   I have thought of that. [*Exit.*]
S.   The little funk. Sunlight on sparkling water, its
        shades dissolved, reforming, unreal activity where
        others laughed but he blubbed clinging, homesick,
        and undeveloped form. I'll do it. Men point in aft-
        er days. He always was. But wrongly. He fought and

[27]

overcame, a stern self-ruler. You didn't hear. Hearing
they look ashamed too late for shaking hands. Of
course I'll do it. [*Exit.*]

[*A shot. More shots. Shouting.*]

Voices outside.   A trap. I might have known.

Take that, damn you.

Open the window.

You swine.

Jimmy, O my God.

[*Enter Seth and Bernard.*]

B.   The Master's killed. So is John Nower, but some of
          them got away, fetching help, will attack in an hour.

S.   See that all the doors are bolted.

[*Exeunt right and left. The back curtains draw. Anne with
the dead.*]

Anne.   Now we have seen the story to its end.
          The hands that were to help will not be lifted,
          And bad followed by worse leaves to us tears,
          An empty bed, hope from less noble men.
          I had seen joy
          Received and given, upon both sides, for years.
          Now not.

*Chorus.*Though he believe it, no man is strong.
          He thinks to be called the fortunate,
          To bring home a wife, to live long.

          But he is defeated; let the son
          Sell the farm lest the mountain fall;
          His mother and her mother won.

          His fields are used up where the moles visit,
          The contours worn flat; if there show
          Passage for water he will miss it:

[28]

Give up his breath, his woman, his team;
No life to touch, though later there be
Big fruit, eagles above the stream.

CURTAIN

POEMS

I

Will you turn a deaf ear
To what they said on the shore,
interrogate their poises
in their rich houses;

Of stork-legged heaven-reachers
Of the compulsory touchers
The sensitive amusers
And masked amazers?

Yet wear no ruffian badge
Nor lie behind the hedge
Waiting with bombs of conspiracy
In arm-pit secrecy;

Carry no talisman
For germ or the abrupt pain
Needing no concrete shelter
Nor porcelain filter.

Will you wheel death anywhere
in his invalid chair,
With no affectionate instant
But his attendant?

For to be held for friend
By an undeveloped mind
To be joke for children is
Death's happiness:

Whose anecdotes betray
His favourite colour as blue
Colour of distant bells
And boys' overalls.

His tales of the bad lands
Disturb the sewing hands;
Hard to be superior
On parting nausea;

To accept the cushions from
Women against martyrdom.
Yet applauding the circuits
Of racing cyclists.

Never to make signs
Fear neither maelstrom nor zones
Salute with soldiers' wives
When the flag waves;

Remembering there is
No recognized gift for this;
No income, no bounty,
No promised country.

But to see brave sent home
Hermetically sealed with shame
And cold's victorious wrestle
With molten metal.

A neutralizing peace
And an average disgrace
Are honour to discover
For later other.

II

Doom is dark and deeper than any sea-dingle.
Upon what man it fall
In spring, day-wishing flowers appearing,
Avalanche sliding, white snow from rock-face,
That he should leave his house,
No cloud-soft hand can hold him, restraint by women;
But ever that man goes
Through place-keepers, through forest trees,
A stranger to strangers over undried sea,
Houses for fishes, suffocating water,
Or lonely on fell as chat,
By pot-holed becks
A bird stone-haunting, an unquiet bird.

There head falls forward, fatigued at evening,
And dreams of home,
Waving from window, spread of welcome,
Kissing of wife under single sheet;
But waking sees
Bird-flocks nameless to him, through doorway voices
Of new men making another love.

Save him from hostile capture,
From sudden tiger's spring at corner;
Protect his house,
His anxious house where days are counted
From thunderbolt protect,
From gradual ruin spreading like a stain;
Converting number from vague to certain,
Bring joy, bring day of his returning,
Lucky with day approaching, with leaning dawn.

III

Since you are going to begin to-day
Let us consider what it is you do.
You are the one whose part it is to lean,
For whom it is not good to be alone.
Laugh warmly turning shyly in the hall
Or climb with bare knees the volcanic hill,
Acquire that flick of wrist and after strain
Relax in your darling's arms like a stone
Remembering everything you can confess,
Making the most of firelight, of hours of fuss;
But joy is mine not yours – to have come so far,
Whose cleverest invention was lately fur;
Lizards my best once who took years to breed,
Could not control the temperature of blood.
To reach that shape for your face to assume,
Pleasure to many and despair to some,
I shifted ranges, lived epochs handicapped
By climate, wars, or what the young men kept,
Modified theories on the types of dross,
Altered desire and history of dress.

You in the town now call the exile fool
That writes home once a year as last leaves fall,
Think – Romans had a language in their day
And ordered roads with it, but it had to die:
Your culture can but leave – forgot as sure
As place-name origins in favourite shire –
Jottings for stories, some often-mentioned Jack,
And references in letters to a private joke,
Equipment rusting in unweeded lanes,
Virtues still advertised on local lines;

And your conviction shall help none to fly,
Cause rather a perversion on next floor.

Nor even is despair your own, when swiftly
Comes general assault on your ideas of safety:
That sense of famine, central anguish felt
For goodness wasted at peripheral fault,
Your shutting up the house and taking prow
To go into the wilderness to pray,
Means that I wish to leave and to pass on,
Select another form, perhaps your son;
Though he reject you, join opposing team
Be late or early at another time,
My treatment will not differ – he will be tipped,
Found weeping, signed for, made to answer, topped.
Do not imagine you can abdicate;
Before you reach the frontier you are caught;
Others have tried it and will try again
To finish that which they did not begin:
Their fate must always be the same as yours,
To suffer the loss they were afraid of, yes,
Holders of one position, wrong for years.

IV

Watch any day his nonchalant pauses, see
His dextrous handling of a wrap as he
Steps after into cars, the beggar's envy.

'There is a free one' many say, but err.
He is not that returning conqueror,
Nor ever the poles' circumnavigator.

But poised between shocking falls on razor-edge
Has taught himself this balancing subterfuge
Of the accosting profile, the erect carriage.

The song, the varied action of the blood
Would drown the warning from the iron wood
Would cancel the inertia of the buried:

Travelling by daylight on from house to house
The longest way to the intrinsic peace,
With love's fidelity and with love's weakness.

V

From the very first coming down
Into a new valley with a frown
Because of the sun and a lost way,
You certainly remain: to-day
I, crouching behind a sheep-pen, heard
Travel across a sudden bird,
Cry out against the storm, and found
The year's arc a completed round
And love's worn circuit re-begun,
Endless with no dissenting turn.
Shall see, shall pass, as we have seen
The swallow on the tile, spring's green
Preliminary shiver, passed
A solitary truck, the last
Of shunting in the Autumn. But now
To interrupt the homely brow,
Thought warmed to evening through and through
Your letter comes, speaking as you,
Speaking of much but not to come.

Nor speech is close nor fingers numb,
If love not seldom has received
An unjust answer, was deceived.
I, decent with the seasons, move
Different or with a different love,
Nor question overmuch the nod,
The stone smile of this country god
That never was more reticent,
Always afraid to say more than it meant.

VI

Between attention and attention
The first and last decision
Is mortal distraction
Of earth and air,
Further and nearer,
The vague wants
Of days and nights,
And personal error;
And the fatigued face.
Taking the strain
Of the horizontal force
And the vertical thrust,
Makes random answer
To the crucial test;
The uncertain flesh
Scraping back chair
For the wrong train,
Falling in slush,
Before a friend's friends
Or shaking hands
With a snub-nosed winner.

The opening window, closing door,
Open, close, but not
To finish or restore;
These wishes get
No further than
The edges of the town,
And leaning asking from the car
Cannot tell us where we are;
While the divided face

Has no grace,
No discretion,
No occupation
But registering
Acreage, mileage,
The easy knowledge
Of the virtuous thing.

VII

Upon this line between adventure
Prolong the meeting out of good nature
Obvious in each agreeable feature.

Calling of each other by name
Smiling, taking a willing arm
Has the companionship of a game.

But should the walk do more than this
Out of bravado or drunkenness
Forward or back are menaces.

On neither side let foot slip over
Invading Always, exploring Never,
For this is hate and this is fear.

On narrowness stand, for sunlight is
Brightest only on surfaces;
No anger, no traitor, but peace.

VIII

Again in conversations
Speaking of fear
And throwing off reserve
The voice is nearer
But no clearer
Than first love
Than boys' imaginations.

For every news
Means pairing off in twos and twos
Another I, another You
Each knowing what to do
But of no use.

Never stronger
But younger and younger
Saying goodbye but coming back, for fear
Is over there
And the centre of anger
Is out of danger.

IX

It's no use raising a shout.
No, Honey, you can cut that right out.
I don't want any more hugs;
Make me some fresh tea, fetch me some rugs.
Here am I, here are you:
But what does it mean? What are we going to do?

A long time ago I told my mother
I was leaving home to find another:
I never answered her letter
But I never found a better.
Here am I, here are you:
But what does it mean? What are we going to do?

It wasn't always like this?
Perhaps it wasn't, but it is.
Put the car away; when life fails,
What's the good of going to Wales?
Here am I, here are you:
But what does it mean? What are we going to do?

In my spine there was a base;
And I knew the general's face:
But they've severed all the wires,
And I can't tell what the general desires.
Here am I, here are you:
But what does it mean? What are we going to do?

In my veins there is a wish,
And a memory of fish:
When I lie crying on the floor,
It says, 'You've often done this before.'
Here am I, here are you:
But what does it mean? What are we going to do?

A bird used to visit this shore:
It isn't going to come any more.
I've come a very long way to prove
No land, no water, and no love.
Here am I, here are you:
But what does it mean? What are we going to do?

X

Love by ambition
Of definition
Suffers partition
And cannot go
From yes to no
For no is not love, no is no
The shutting of a door
The tightening jaw
A conscious sorrow,
And saying yes
Turns love into success
Views from the rail
Of land and happiness,
Assured of all
The sofas creak
And were this all, love were
But cheek to cheek
And dear to dear.

Voices explain
Love's pleasure and love's pain
Still tap the knee
And cannot disagree
Hushed for aggression
Of full confession
Likeness to likeness
Of each old weakness;
Love is not there
Love has moved to another chair.

Aware already
Of who stands next
And is not vexed
And is not giddy
Leaves the North in place
With a good grace
And would not gather
Another to another
Designs his own unhappiness
Foretells his own death and is faithless.

XI

Who stands, the crux left of the watershed,
On the wet road between the chafing grass
Below him sees dismantled washing-floors,
Snatches of tramline running to the wood,
An industry already comatose,
Yet sparsely living. A ramshackle engine
At Cashwell raises water; for ten years
It lay in flooded workings until this,
Its latter office, grudgingly performed;
And further here and there, though many dead
Lie under the poor soil, some acts are chosen
Taken from recent winters; two there were
Cleaned out a damaged shaft by hand, clutching
The winch the gale would tear them from; one died
During a storm, the fells impassable,
Not at his village, but in wooden shape
Through long abandoned levels nosed his way
And in his final valley went to ground.

Go home, now, stranger, proud of your young stock,
Stranger, turn back again, frustrate and vexed:
This land, cut off, will not communicate,
Be no accessory content to one
Aimless for faces rather there than here.
Beams from your car may cross a bedroom wall,
They wake no sleeper; you may hear the wind
Arriving driven from the ignorant sea
To hurt itself on pane, on bark of elm
Where sap unbaffled rises, being spring;
But seldom this. Near you, taller than grass,
Ears poise before decision, scenting danger.

XII

We made all possible preparations,
Drew up a list of firms,
Constantly revised our calculations
And allotted the farms,

Issued all the orders expedient
In this kind of case:
Most, as was expected, were obedient,
Though there were murmurs, of course;

Chiefly against our exercising
Our old right to abuse:
Even some sort of attempt at rising
But these were mere boys.

For never serious misgiving
Occurred to anyone,
Since there could be no question of living
If we did not win.

The generally accepted view teaches
That there was no excuse,
Though in the light of recent researches
Many would find the cause

In a not uncommon form of terror;
Others, still more astute,
Point to possibilities of error
At the very start.

As for ourselves there is left remaining
Our honour at least,
And a reasonable chance of retaining
Our faculties to the last.

[49]

XIII

What's in your mind, my dove, my coney;
Do thoughts grow like feathers, the dead end of life;
Is it making of love or counting of money,
Or raid on the jewels, the plans of a thief?

Open your eyes, my dearest dallier;
Let hunt with your hands for escaping me;
Go through the motions of exploring the familiar
Stand on the brink of the warm white day.

Rise with the wind, my great big serpent;
Silence the birds and darken the air;
Change me with terror, alive in a moment;
Strike for the heart and have me there.

XIV

Sentries against inner and outer,
At stated interval is feature;
And how shall enemy on these
Make sudden raid or lasting peace?
For bribery were vain to try
Against the incorruptible eye
Too amply paid with tears, the chin
Has hairs to hide its weakness in,
And proud bridge and indignant nostril
Nothing to do but to look noble.
But in between these lies the mouth;
Watch that, that you may parley with:
There strategy comes easiest,
Though it seem stern, was seen compressed
Over a lathe, refusing answer,
It will release the ill-fed prisoner
It will do murder or betray
For either party equally,
Yielding at last to a close kiss
It will admit tongue's soft advance,
So longed for, given in abandon,
Given long since, had it but known.

XV

Control of the passes was, he saw, the key
To this new district, but who would get it?
He, the trained spy, had walked into the trap
For a bogus guide, seduced with the old tricks.

At Greenhearth was a fine site for a dam
And easy power, had they pushed the rail
Some stations nearer. They ignored his wires.
The bridges were unbuilt and trouble coming.

The street music seemed gracious now to one
For weeks up in the desert. Woken by water
Running away in the dark, he often had
Reproached the night for a companion
Dreamed of already. They would shoot, of course,
Parting easily who were never joined.

XVI

It was Easter as I walked in the public gardens
Hearing the frogs exhaling from the pond,
Watching traffic of magnificent cloud
Moving without anxiety on open sky –
Season when lovers and writers find
An altering speech for altering things,
An emphasis on new names, on the arm
A fresh hand with fresh power.
But thinking so I came at once
Where solitary man sat weeping on a bench,
Hanging his head down, with his mouth distorted
Helpless and ugly as an embryo chicken.

So I remember all of those whose death
Is necessary condition of the season's setting forth,
Who sorry in this time look only back
To Christmas intimacy, a winter dialogue
Fading in silence, leaving them in tears.
And recent particulars come to mind;
The death by cancer of a once hated master,
A friend's analysis of his own failure,
Listened to at intervals throughout the winter
At different hours and in different rooms.
But always with success of others for comparison,
The happiness, for instance, of my friend Kurt Groote,
Absence of fear in Gerhart Meyer
From the sea, the truly strong man.

A 'bus ran home then, on the public ground
Lay fallen bicycles like huddled corpses:

No chattering valves of laughter emphasized
Nor the swept gown ends of a gesture stirred
The sessile hush; until a sudden shower
Fell willing into grass and closed the day,
Making choice seem a necessary error.

2

Coming out of me living is always thinking,
Thinking changing and changing living,
Am feeling as it was seeing –
In city leaning on harbour parapet
To watch a colony of duck below
Sit, preen, and doze on buttresses
Or upright paddle on flickering stream,
Casually fishing at a passing straw.
Those find sun's luxury enough,
Shadow know not of homesick foreigner
Nor restlessness of intercepted growth.

All this time was anxiety at night,
Shooting and barricade in street.
Walking home late I listened to a friend
Talking excitedly of final war
Of proletariat against police –
That one shot girl of nineteen through the knees
They threw that one down concrete stair –
Till I was angry, said I was pleased.

Time passes in Hessen, in Gutensberg,
With hill-top and evening holds me up,
Tiny observer of enormous world.
Smoke rises from factory in field,
Memory of fire: On all sides heard
Vanishing music of isolated larks:

From village square voices in hymn,
Men's voices, an old use.
And I above standing, saying in thinking:

'Is first baby, warm in mother,
Before born and is still mother,
Time passes and now is other,
Is knowledge in him now of other,
Cries in cold air, himself no friend.
In grown man also, may see in face
In his day-thinking and in his night-thinking
Is wareness and is fear of other,
Alone in flesh, himself no friend.

He say 'We must forgive and forget,'
Forgetting saying but is unforgiving
And unforgiving is in his living;
Body reminds in him to loving,
Reminds but takes no further part,
Perfunctorily affectionate in hired room
But takes no part and is unloving
But loving death. May see in dead,
In face of dead that loving wish,
As one returns from Africa to wife
And his ancestral property in Wales.'

Yet sometimes man look and say good
At strict beauty of locomotive,
Completeness of gesture or unclouded eye;
In me so absolute unity of evening
And field and distance was in me for peace,
Was over me in feeling without forgetting
Those ducks' indifference, that friend's hysteria,
Without wishing and with forgiving,

To love my life, not as other,
Not as bird's life, not as child's,
'Cannot,' I said, 'being no child now nor a bird.'

3

Order to stewards and the study of time,
Correct in books, was earlier than this
But joined this by the wires I watched from train,
slackening of wire and posts' sharp reprimand,
In month of August to a cottage coming.

Being alone, the frightened soul
Returns to this life of sheep and hay
No longer his: he every hour
Moves further from this and must so move,
As child is weaned from his mother and leaves home
But taking the first steps falters, is vexed,
Happy only to find home, a place
Where no tax is levied for being there.

So, insecure, he loves and love
Is insecure, gives less than he expects.
He knows not if it be seed in time to display
Luxuriantly in a wonderful fructification
Or whether it be but a degenerate remnant
Of something immense in the past but now
Surviving only as the infectiousness of disease
Or in the malicious caricature of drunkenness;
Its end glossed over by the careless but known long
To finer perception of the mad and ill.

Moving along the track which is himself,
He loves what he hopes will last, which gone,
Begins the difficult work of mourning,

And as foreign settlers to strange county come,
By mispronunciation of native words
And by intermarriage create a new race
And a new language, so may the soul
Be weaned at last to independent delight.

Startled by the violent laugh of a jay
I went from wood, from crunch underfoot,
Air between stems as under water;
As I shall leave the summer, see autumn come
Focussing stars more sharply in the sky,
See frozen buzzard flipped down the weir
And carried out to sea, leave autumn,
See winter, winter for earth and us,
A forethought of death that we may find ourselves
        at death
Not helplessly strange to the new conditions.

4

It is time for the destruction of error.
The chairs are being brought in from the garden,
The summer talk stopped on that savage coast
Before the storms, after the guests and birds:
In sanatoriums they laugh less and less,
Less certain of cure; and the loud madman
Sinks now into a more terrible calm.

The falling leaves know it, the children,
At play on the fuming alkali-tip
Or by the flooded football ground, know it –
This is the dragon's day, the devourer's:
Orders are given to the enemy for a time
With underground proliferation of mould,
With constant whisper and the casual question,

To haunt the poisoned in his shunned house,
To destroy the efflorescence of the flesh,
The intricate play of the mind, to enforce
Conformity with the orthodox bone,
With organized fear, the articulated skeleton.

You whom I gladly walk with, touch,
Or wait for as one certain of good,
We know it, we know that love
Needs more than the admiring excitement of union,
More than the abrupt self-confident farewell,
The heel on the finishing blade of grass,
The self-confidence of the falling root,
Needs death, death of the grain, our death,
Death of the old gang; would leave them
In sullen valley where is made no friend,
The old gang to be forgotten in the spring,
The hard bitch and the riding-master,
Stiff underground; deep in clear lake
The lolling bridegroom, beautiful, there.

XVII

This lunar beauty
Has no history
Is complete and early;
If beauty later
Bear any feature
It had a lover
And is another.

This like a dream
Keeps other time
And daytime is
The loss of this;
For time is inches
And the heart's changes
Where ghost has haunted
Lost and wanted.

But this was never
A ghost's endeavour
Nor finished this,
Was ghost at ease;
And till it pass
Love shall not near
The sweetness here
Nor sorrow take
His endless look.

XVIII

Before this loved one
Was that one and that one
A family
And history
And ghost's adversity
Whose pleasing name
Was neighbourly shame.
Before this last one
Was much to be done,
Frontiers to cross
As clothes grew worse
And coins to pass
In a cheaper house
Before this last one
Before this loved one.

Face that the sun
Is supple on
May stir but here
Is no new year;
This gratitude for gifts is less
Than the old loss;
Touching is shaking hands
On mortgaged lands;
And smiling of
This gracious greeting
'Good day. Good luck'
Is no real meeting
But instinctive look
A backward love.

XIX

The silly fool, the silly fool
Was sillier in school
But beat the bully as a rule.

The youngest son, the youngest son
Was certainly no wise one
Yet could surprise one.

Or rather, or rather
To be posh, we gather,
One should have no father.

Simple to prove
That deeds indeed
In life succeed
But love in love
And tales in tales
Where no one fails.

XX

The strings' excitement, the applauding drum
Are but the initiating ceremony
That out of cloud the ancestral face may come.

And never hear their subaltern mockery,
Graphiti-writers, moss-grown with whimsies,
Loquacious when the watercourse is dry.

It is your face I see, and morning's praise
Of you is ghost's approval of the choice,
Filtered through roots of the effacing grass.

Fear, taking me aside, would give advice
'To conquer her, the visible enemy,
it is enough to turn away the eyes.'

Yet there's no peace in this assaulted city
But speeches at the corners, hope for news,
Outside the watchfires of a stronger army.

And all emotions to expression came,
Recovering the archaic imagery:
This longing for assurance takes the form

Of a hawk's vertical stooping from the sky;
These tears, salt for a disobedient dream,
The lunatic agitation of the sea;

While this despair with hardened eyeballs cries
'A Golden Age, a Silver . . . rather this,
Massive and taciturn years, the Age of Ice.'

XXI

On Sunday walks
Past the shut gates of works
The conquerors come
And are handsome.

Sitting all day
By the open window
Say what they say
Know what to know
Who brought and taught
Unusual images
And new tunes to old cottages,
With so much done
Without a thought
Of the anonymous lampoon
The cellar counterplot,
Though in the night
Pursued by eaters
They clutch at gaiters
That straddle and deny
Escape that way,
Though in the night
Is waking fright.

Father by son
Lives on and on
Though over date
And motto on the gate
The lichen grows
From year to year,
Still here and there

That Roman nose
Is noticed in the villages
And father's son
Knows what they said
And what they did.

Not meaning to deceive,
Wish to give suck
Enforces make-believe
And what was fear
Of fever and bad-luck
Is now a scare
At certain names
A need for charms
For certain words
At certain fords
And what was livelihood
Is tallness, strongness
Words and longness,
All glory and all story
Solemn and not so good.

XXII

Get there if you can and see the land you once were proud
 to own
Though the roads have almost vanished and the expresses
 never run:

Smokeless chimneys, damaged bridges, rotting wharves and
 choked canals,
Tramlines buckled, smashed trucks lying on their side across
 the rails;

Power-stations locked, deserted, since they drew the boiler
 fires;
Pylons fallen or subsiding, trailing dead high-tension wires;

Head-gears gaunt on grass-grown pit-banks, seams
 abandoned years ago;
Drop a stone and listen for its splash in flooded dark below.

Squeeze into the works through broken windows or through
 damp-sprung doors;
See the rotted shafting, see holes gaping in the upper floors;

Where the Sunday lads come talking motor bicycle and girl,
Smoking cigarettes in chains until their heads are in a whirl.

Far from there we spent the money, thinking we could well
 afford,
While they quietly undersold us with their cheaper trade
 abroad;

At the theatre, playing tennis, driving motor cars we had,
In our continental villas, mixing cocktails for a cad.

These were boon companions who devised the legends for
    our tombs,
These who have betrayed us nicely while we took them to
    our rooms.

Newman, Ciddy, Plato, Fronny, Pascal, Bowdler, Baudelaire,
Doctor Frommer, Mrs Allom, Freud, the Baron, and
    Flaubert.

Lured with their compelling logic, charmed with beauty of
    their verse,
With their loaded sideboards whispered 'Better join us, life is
    worse.'

Taught us at the annual camps arranged by the big business
    men
'Sunbathe, pretty till you're twenty. You shall be our
    servants then.'

Perfect pater. Marvellous mater. Knock the critic down who
    dares –
Very well, believe it, copy; till your hair is white as theirs.

Yours you say were parents to avoid, avoid then if you please
Do the reverse on all occasion till you catch the same
    disease.

When we asked the way to Heaven, these directed us ahead
To the padded room, the clinic and the hangman's little shed.

Intimate as war-time prisoners in an isolation camp,
Living month by month together, nervy, famished, lousy,
    damp.

On the sopping esplanade or from our dingy lodgings we
Stare out dully at the rain which falls for miles into the sea.

Lawrence, Blake and Homer Lane, once healers in our
       English land;
These are dead as iron for ever; these can never hold our
       hand.

Lawrence was brought down by smut-hounds, Blake went
       dotty as he sang,
Homer Lane was killed in action by the Twickenham Baptist
       gang.

Have things gone too far already? Are we done for? Must we
       wait
Hearing doom's approaching footsteps regular down miles
       of straight;

Run the whole night through in gumboots, stumble on and
       gasp for breath,
Terrors drawing close and closer, winter landscape, fox's
       death;

Or, in friendly fireside circle, sit and listen for the crash
Meaning that the mob has realized something's up, and start
       to smash;

Engine-drivers with their oil-cans, factory girls in overalls
Blowing sky-high monster stores, destroying intellectuals?

Hope and fear are neck and neck: which is it near the
       course's end
Crashes, having lost his nerve; is overtaken on the bend?

Shut up talking, charming in the best suits to be had in
       town,
Lecturing on navigation while the ship is going down.

Drop those priggish ways for ever, stop behaving like a
    stone:
Throw the bath-chairs right away, and learn to leave
    ourselves alone.

If we really want to live, we'd better start at once to try;
If we don't, it doesn't matter, but we'd better start to die.

XXIII

Look there! The sunk road winding
To the fortified farm.
Listen! The cock's alarm
In the strange valley.

Are we the stubborn athletes;
Are we then to begin
The run between the gin
And bloody falcon?

The horns of the dark squadron
Converging to attack;
The sound behind our back
Of glaciers calving.

In legend all were simple,
And held the staitened spot;
But we in legend not,
Are not simple.

In weakness how much further;
Along what crooked route
By hedgehog's gradual foot,
Or fish's fathom.

Bitter the blue smoke rises
From garden bonfires lit,
To where we burning sit:
Good, if it's thorough.

It won't be us who eavesdrop
In days of luck and heat,
Timing the double beat
At last together.

XXIV

From scars where kestrels hover,
The leader looking over
Into the happy valley,
Orchard and curving river,
May turn away to see
The slow fastidious line
That disciplines the fell,
Hear curlew's creaking call
From angles unforseen,
The drumming of a snipe
Surprise where driven sleet
Had scalded to the bone
And streams are acrid yet
To an unaccustomed lip.
The tall unwounded leader
Of doomed companions, all
Whose voices in the rock
Are now perpetual,
Fighters for no one's sake,
Who died beyond the border.

Heroes are buried who
Did not believe in death
And bravery is now
Not in the dying breath
But resisting the temptations
To skyline operations.

Yet glory is not new;
The summer visitors
Still come from far and wide,

Choosing their spots to view
The prize competitors,
Each thinking that he will
Find heroes in the wood,
Far from the capital

Where lights and wine are set
For supper by the lake,
But leaders must migrate:
'Leave for Cape Wrath to-night,'
And the host after waiting
Must quench the lamps and pass
Alive into the house.

XXV

Who will endure
Heat of day and winter danger,
Journey from one place to another?
Nor be content to lie
Till evening upon headland over bay,
Between the land and sea;
Or smoking wait till hour of food,
Leaning on chained-up gate
At edge of wood.

Metals run
Burnished or rusty in the sun
From town to town,
And signals all along are down;
Yet nothing passes
But envelopes between these places,
Snatched at the gate and panting read indoors,
And first spring flowers arriving smashed,
Disaster stammered over wires,
And pity flashed.
For should professional traveller come,
Asked at the fireside he is dumb,
Declining with a small mad smile,
And all the while
Conjectures on the maps that lie
About in ships long high and dry
Grow stranger and stranger.

There is no change of place
But shifting of the head
To keep off glare of lamp from face,

Or climbing over to wall-side of bed;
No one will ever know
For what conversion brilliant capital is waiting,
What ugly feast may village band be celebrating;
For no one goes
Further than railhead or the ends of piers,
Will neither go nor send his son
Further through foothills than the rotting stack
Where gaitered gamekeeper with dog and gun
Will shout 'Turn back'.

XXVI

Taller to-day, we remember similar evenings,
Walking together in the windless orchard
Where the brook runs over the gravel, far from the glacier.

Again in the room with the sofa hiding the grate,
Look down to the river when the rain is over,
See him turn to the window, hearing our last
Of Captain Ferguson.

It is seen how excellent hands have turned to commonness.
One staring too long, went blind in a tower,
One sold all his manors to fight, broke through, and faltered.

Nights come bringing the snow, and the dead howl
Under the headlands in their windy dwelling
Because the Adversary put too easy questions
On lonely roads.

But happy now, though no nearer each other,
We see the farms lighted all along the valley;
Down at the mill-shed the hammering stops
And men go home.

Noises at dawn will bring
Freedom for some, but not this peace
No bird can contradict: passing, but is sufficient now
For something fulfilled this hour, loved or endured.

XXVII

To ask the hard question is simple;
Asking at meeting
With the simple glance of acquaintance
To what these go
And how these do:
To ask the hard question is simple,
The simple act of the confused will.

But the answer
Is hard and hard to remember:
On steps or on shore
The ears listening
To words at meeting,
The eyes looking
At the hands helping,
Are never sure
Of what they learn
From how these things are done.
And forgetting to listen or see
Makes forgetting easy;
Only remembering the method of remembering,
Remembering only in another way,
Only the strangely exciting lie,
Afraid
To remember what the fish ignored,
How the bird escaped, or if the sheep obeyed.

Till, losing memory,
Bird, fish, and sheep are ghostly,
And ghosts must do again
What gives them pain.

Cowardice cries
For windy skies,
Coldness for water,
Obedience for a master.

Shall memory restore
The steps and the shore,
The face and the meeting place;
Shall the bird live,
Shall the fish dive,
And sheep obey
In a sheep's way;
Can love remember
The question and the answer,
For love recover
What has been dark and rich and warm all over?

XXVIII

Under boughs between our tentative endearments how
     should we hear
But with flushing pleasure drums distant over difficult
     country,
          Events not actual
          In time's unlenient will?

Which we shall not avoid, though at a station's chance delay
Lines branch to peace, iron up valleys to a hidden village;
          For we have friends to catch
          And none leave coach.

Sharers of our own day, thought smiling of, but nothing
     known,
What industries decline, what chances are of revolution,
          What murders flash
          Under composed flesh.

Knowledge no need to us whose wrists enjoy the chafing
     leash,
Can plunder high nests; who sheer off from old like gull
     from granite,
          From their mind's constant sniffling,
          Their blood's dulled shuffling.

Who feebling, still have time to wonder at the well-shaped
     heads
Conforming every day more closely to the best in albums:
          Fathers in sons may track
          Their voices trick.

But their ancestral curse, jumbled perhaps and put away,
Baffled for years, at last in one repeats its potent pattern
       And blows fall more than once,
       Although he wince:

Who was to moorland market town retired for work or love,
May creep to sumps, pile up against the door, crouching
    in cases,
       This anger falling
       Opens, empties that filling.

Let each one share our pity, hard to withhold and hard to
    bear.
None knows of the next day if it be less or more, the sorrow:
       Escaping cannot try;
       Must wait though it destroy.

XXIX

Consider this and in our time
As the hawk sees it or the helmeted airman:
The clouds rift suddenly – look there
At cigarette-end smouldering on a border
At the first garden party of the year.
Pass on, admire the view of the massif
Through plate-glass windows of the Sport Hotel;
Join there the insufficient units
Dangerous, easy, in furs, in uniform
And constellated at reserved tables
Supplied with feelings by an efficient band
Relayed elsewhere to farmers and their dogs
Sitting in kitchens in the stormy fens.

Long ago, supreme Antagonist,
More powerful than the great northern whale
Ancient and sorry at life's limiting defect,
In Cornwall, Mendip, or the Pennine moor
Your comments on the highborn mining-captains,
Found they no answer, made them wish to die
– Lie since in barrows out of harm.
You talk to your admirers every day
By silted harbours, derelict works,
In strangled orchards, and the silent comb
Where dogs have worried or a bird was shot.
Order the ill that they attack at once:
Visit the ports and, interrupting
The leisurely conversation in the bar
Within a stone's throw of the sunlit water,
Beckon your chosen out. Summon
Those handsome and diseased youngsters, those women

Your solitary agents in the country parishes;
And mobilize the powerful forces latent
In soils that make the farmer brutal
In the infected sinus, and the eyes of stoats.
Then, ready, start your rumour, soft
But horrifying in its capacity to disgust
Which, spreading magnified, shall come to
A polar peril, a prodigious alarm,
Scattering the people, as torn-up paper
Rags and utensils in a sudden gust,
Seized with immeasurable neurotic dread.

Financier, leaving your little room
Where the money is made but not spent,
You'll need your typist and your boy no more;
The game is up for you and for the others,
Who, thinking, pace in slippers on the lawns
Of College Quad or Cathedral Close,
Who are born nurses, who live in shorts
Sleeping with people and playing fives.
Seekers after happiness, all who follow
The convolutions of your simple wish,
It is later than you think; nearer that day
Far other than that distant afternoon
Amid rustle of frocks and stamping feet
They gave the prizes to the ruined boys.
You cannot be away, then, no
Not though you pack to leave within an hour,
Escaping humming down arterial roads:
The date was yours; the prey to fugues,
Irregular breathing and alternate ascendancies
After some haunted migratory years
To disintegrate on an instant in the explosion of mania
Or lapse for ever into a classic fatigue.

XXX

Sir, no man's enemy, forgiving all
But will his negative inversion, be prodigal:
Send to us power and light, a sovereign touch
Curing the intolerable neural itch,
The exhaustion of weaning, the liar's quinsy,
And the distortions of ingrown virginity.
Prohibit sharply the rehearsed response
And gradually correct the coward's stance;
Cover in time with beams those in retreat
That, spotted, they turn though the reverse were great;
Publish each healer that in city lives
Or country houses at the end of drives;
Harrow the house of the dead; look shining at
New styles of architecture, a change of heart.